(gentlessness)

Also by Dan Beachy-Quick

Poetry

North True South Bright
Spell
Mulberry
This Nest, Swift Passerine
Circle's Apprentice

Collaborations

Work From Memory: In Response to In Search of Lost Time by
    Marcel Proust (with Matthew Goulish)
Conversities (with Srikanth Reddy)

Chapbooks (with poems not collected in books)

Apology for the Book of Creatures
Shields & Shards & Stitches & Songs

Essays

A Whaler's Dictionary
Wonderful Investigations: Essays, Meditations, Tales
A Brighter Word than Bright: Keats at Work

Novel

An Impenetrable Screen of Purest Sky

(gentlessness)

Poems

Dan Beachy-Quick

T|P

TUPELO PRESS
North Adams, Massachusetts

gentlessness.

Library of Congress Cataloging-in-Publication Data

Beachy-Quick, Dan, 1973-
  [Poems. Selections]
  gentlessness : poems / Dan Beachy-Quick. -- First paperback edition.
    pages cm
  ISBN 978-1-936797-57-8 (pbk. : alk. paper)
  I. Title.
  PS3602.E24A6 2015
  811ʹ.6--dc23
          2015000188

Cover and text designed by Howard Klein.

Cover art: Jess, *Hera Closing with Herakles* (1960), collage, 19 ½ x 23 ½
inches. Private Collection. Copyright © The Jess Collins Trust and used by
permission, with courtesy of Tibor de Nagy Gallery, New York.

First paperback edition: April 2015.

Tupelo Press
P.O. Box 1767, North Adams, Massachusetts 01247
Telephone: (413) 664-9611 / editor@tupelopress.org / www.tupelopress.org

Tupelo Press is an award-winning independent literary press that publishes
fine fiction, nonfiction, and poetry in books that are a joy to hold as well as
read. Tupelo Press is a registered 501(c)(3) nonprofit organization, and we
rely on public support to carry out our mission of publishing extraordinary
work that may be outside the realm of the large commercial publishers.
Financial donations are welcome and are tax deductible.

ART WORKS.
arts.gov

Supported in part by an award from the National Endowment for the Arts

for Kristy, Hana, Iris—

O fret not after knowledge — I have none,
And yet my song comes native with the warmth.
O fret not after knowledge — I have none,
And yet the Evening listens.

Contents

I am alive as long as I have fire in my head

and sing for my supper, out of the mouth of the dead

—Ronald Johnson, BEAM 8

I sing to praise their song.

—William Bronk

monadism: a proem

1.

that that what is is an all

*

all filled with what all fills it

*

please plenum appease o

*

certain adam among the abstract all

2.

at every point every line meets every

*

word wears a mirror for a face

*

what is complex is underneath the image

*

it knows more than it shows

3.

soul so simple a sense

*

desires as a stone desires to fall

*

so quick into the center of what

*

we call whole or world

4.

a fragment acts flagrant but is not

*

fragrance of rose where every rose is

*

o soul so full of souls

*

the only secret is there is none

5.

no real release there is

*

some subtle error in prayer

*

see a word to read what it is

*

a word sees all this nothing it seeks

6.

sing me open to swerve error astray

*

but prayer makes a point inside

*

of infinite angles so sin learns

*

a song to sing o source asleep

7.

desire or at least constant disquiet

*

body real as is a rainbow real

*

a certain perfection perfectly uncertain

*

nonce spectra the unfolding soul elates

8.

as in a kind of center called belief

*

a center none can find nor none prove

*

faith's fatal point

*

accept the void and the atoms

a short treatise on the nature of the gods

1.

Earth in the deepening groove
Some mind's coruscation   the sun
On the blue water fleshes out
The face gathers around a voice

2.

Every day a snake eats its own head.
Night is the eyes in the mouth.

Remember to forget to remember
Everything known. Day is

What swallows itself.

3.

Around every circle another circle

Thumbprint, thumbnail's half
Moon, orbits of

                        eyes

We say they have eyes   the sun is a

Proof

Looking at us   because we look

4.

. . . give names to what   to that which we
Place names on   empty

Spaces we call some forms of blankness
Ideas   and others we call   pages

. . . call the intimate convergences   you
Where no you is   there is a hope

You exist so we name you   you
Hoping you return   to what

To that which   we call   empty spaces
Some of them   these ideas of   ourselves

5.

Wash out the mouth
Of plurals   false pantheon

Teeth strung across   there

Is no we   only a them

Those pearls

6.

Of wisdom

It steps armored out of the head
And commits itself

To battle
Itself and teaches us to prize

The self-made wound
By displaying its purple bruise

7.

I lay down on my shadow
To imagine myself
As the gods lay down on me
To imagine

I lay down at which time the temple
Snakes cleaned out my ears

I could hear my own future
Though I could not believe

My feet standing on my head
I could bend over so far backward

8.

Face   the violent fact

These wounds are for knowing, these human wounds

The gods have faces but no wounds
The light that pierces our eyes is light
Emitted from their own

We think them but they are thoughtless—

Then the thunder laughs when they close their eyes
And they clap their hands like infants

9.

Not belief but doubt that confirms

Startle the ground-dwelling dove from her gleaning
Her warning call is not her song, but
Air pushed out from her wings' frightened beating

10.

She collects the sea
In a pitcher, she of the prismatic
Wings, a kind of

Messenger, she waters the clouds

Yes, those are rainbows largely
Flapping behind her

Your eyes have not tricked you again

Your eyes whose colored rings we call

Witness a circular fact

Witness a fact turning in a circle ·

11.

Now

No one denies now is when now is

What exists by not existing   the field

      An unfurling pasture whose long grasses are their beds
      Whose wind-swirling grasses is their hair their own
      Fingers twist through

I spoke a prayer   let me inside
                the syllable
                   as I speak it   I spoke a prayer

(I do see that green light and that laughter wild I hear)

12.

Their minds   intestinal

13.

Light feeds them   this light

They eat with their eyes   they stare at the sun

With mouths open   a kind of awe, if

Awe is for them where shadows gather

14.

. . . discussing among themselves the nature of the day:

An hour, what is an hour?
A flower, what is a flower?

What is a bird
Flying with a strand of dead
Grass in her beak? What is a bird

Eating a line?

15.

Ignorance is their nest
Their eyes are on fire
Consume a page or consume
A field they eat with eyes
What they understand is it

16.

"To abolish distance kills. The gods only die by being
among us."

17.

In the atoms beneath logic, in the logic-clouds
Lightning strikes itself to see itself

The accidental particulars   world

World   and one other

Secret is they hide inside us to keep away

Laughter in the fact stirs the fundament

18.

These shadows walk around within me
Dropping grain in the holes of
My eyes don't help the work being open

These shadows step nearer to disappear
And of the blade of wheat sprouting out
My eyes pointing at myself is the answer

19.

The gods tell one joke over and over

Again, "A man walks"

20.

A god walks into a man and the palsy begins
A palsy some call knowing

Intimacy none ask for but none ask for

Release the leaf that in the hand trembles
Is the example of a terrifying wind

Blowing only on the inside, blowing only within

21.

Please the atom to pleasure the god

This point surrounds
Nothing makes of itself a future

Sound of which logic is the magic
Regime and the world a gathering cloud

22.

"A Letter is a joy of Earth—
It is denied the Gods—"

23.

Unfold the fold and find
Another fold below, dark
Mine I call mine when I lie

Ink and mind, ink or mind
The letter forms but it denies
What it finds, the gods are

Dumb because they are wise,
This shadow is the bruise
Of the object's surprise

24.

What laughs inside the flame?

To move the light around
Produces shame
In both the seer and the seen
Shadows move elsewhere

To prove they remain

25.

Step out, step out
Of the cloud and let me see you, step

Out, out
As out of moist earth the mushroom steps, step
As steps the dropped spoor out from under its own head,

Step as a cloud steps down from the open blue
Sky, step down, step

Down and disperse

26.

It wears a groove
Around its head
The song being sung

We singers sing
Of you as we begin,
Of you we singers

Sing as we end

Where weight has been
There is a groove
That binds the head

And singing makes
The groove shudder

27.

Invoke the gods to scare the gods
A song tears them apart
As lightning tears a cloud or as a spider
In an abandoned well tears apart
The stones by linking stone to stone

Threaten them with praise and they will
Pollinate the sun with gnats
Whose clear bodies eat the sun and shit
The sun and make of the road a solar ode

Write an ode and evict the gods, O gods
And goddesses, hear my voice and lean out
Just a little, and give my song light, so what
Is blank is seen, O lean over and give
My song melody, so what is seen
Won't fall apart, O lean out, you gods
And goddesses, and live in the song,
O live in the song, and not in me.

28.

Fragment

A fragment-hymn more

Whole than the whole hymn

... *O, lovely past[ures* ...

heroisms

1.

The hero comes home!—the jerk
In his journeys

His penis grown so long he loops it through
His belt-loops to keep his pants up
And still its tip drags in the dust behind him

Drawing a line pointing backward
To everything the hero's entered. It's a kind of pride:

Origin, that voice
The brute severed from its face, saying as if

Saying forever
"Now crowd yourself back into time."

2.

Do the trick again where you throw your voice
Do that trick

    Where you make the stone say "life is so hard"

    That trick that makes the dead laugh so hard

    That makes the stones follow you as you walk

    The applause that is those tears in the sockets

Do the trick where you put your voice inside the head
Of one who has no voice, that one through whose mouth

You speak to yourself   *golden-sandaled, purple-robed,*
Descend you, descend you whom I love

3.

Nice to walk on the tops of their heads

But hard to keep balance. There are other tricks
The crowd applauds with their hands

As the flower swallows its own head
A green sword cuts itself in half
So a tendril somersaults into a seed

       But you can't bury yourself

Fate rings a bell when the air is on fire
Everyone can breathe fire

       But can you stop breathing
       He says, until the sky turns blue

Inhaling

4.

I speak these words directly into his yawn

Open cave of
          his dark almost kind
                   of fire-lit mouth

And the shadows there my words form
These shadows in the back of the hero's throat

We watch the trees walk past us and want to clap and clap
Except the chains are so loud when we move
We're all afraid the leaves will grow afraid

There are other ways to describe the year:

Acrobat bent so far backward he stands on his own head, or

Seasons of
The hero's boredom

5.

Where the horror is comparison, honor sees
Hands in the trees instead of leaves—

Honesty asks why the applause is so quiet
When the wind blows so hard—

Breath is the atmosphere at utmost extreme
Where the lungs are flowers—thought the dew—

The sun doubts everything, a general statement
In whose light the hero sees these helpless things

Beg mercy, beg darkness for obscurity—
We do not comprehend the awe, it comprehends us—

When leaves fold in halves they look sleepy
Like eyes, but these eyes are fists

6.

What he desires is a face he can desire
Without waking up or changing his own face
But desire puts on him a mask he cannot take off
No matter how he strains the flowers laugh
As he pulls on his ears with all his might

The flowers clap and show him patience
A bee gathering pollen from their dust-heavy eyes
As the hero wrestles his face into the ground

7.

The mirror in his own house kept tricking him
Putting a hole in solid
In solid stone the apple tree bloomed
And the glimmer turning poppy in the sky
He calls the sun my poppy
When the sun is in his house only another room
He feels this awe when he steps forward and sees
His face feeling a shape called awe

8.

The palace is nervous
Her fingers shake holding up her head
The light never veil enough to hide her many eyes

Every door is the erotic entry
Into the underworld
The hero laughs as he gropes Wisdom

Says hard things go soft and World says
Soft things get hard

Faces, facts, columns, flowers, eyes

9.

He carries in his face an infant almost
Always crying

Witness behind the sham veil

Deception is the form description takes
When a tree falls to its knees and begs

For a form called mercy the hero
Feels a form called structure or pride

10.

Speaks about himself to experience
Himself in words others gave him
But uttered deeds grow dark so dark
Clouds stutter and swarm around him
Removing him from himself the hero
Fears he his own frustrated battle
And the field is an audience inside him

11.

Name never subtle he invokes himself

The weather like a riddle he never stops
Asking for an answer instead of a process

(a cloud hides itself in its own display)

Divergent emergencies can split his thunder
Head in two, one voice saying to the other

Its typical lament: "I could'a been a source"

12.

Growing aged and dying
One head became hundreds of
The hero's most feared
Weapon he released with his breath
Alone conquered the empty
Field didn't know it was under attack

13.

Dandelion, you sphinx
You riddle the epic you sing

Bind me fast is the lover's prayer
But the hero's lash is dispersal

14.

He weds Circumference
So abandonment steps
Him always closer home

A center is a simple wreck
Impossible not to believe
The heart is a thing that beats

Beats in the air a ripple
As water beats out from stone
Tears what the hero follows

It rips through the ground
His bride leaves
A furrow in his brow

15.

Circumference is that half-erotic everywhere
That makes the hero go hard

Betrayal a turned-around faithfulness
Abandons the center to prove the orb

16.

There is a way to think that asks no questions
But divides every question in two

The peach splits apart and reveals
Its mind, the crenellated pit

The hero swallows whole each seed
His intestines consider gardens

17.

When he belches the clouds congest

Shamelessness is a stunt they all appreciate
Those bones with the marrow dry inside them
Those sockets in the shoulders all of them in the eyes

When he farts the wrens begin
To sing as he scratches himself

He says, "Look at me, I'm a waterfall . . . "

And the chorus is left behind to gather the wet
Pansies removed from his care and/or thought

" . . . yet this is only half the truth,"

And then he puts the waterfall away

18.

Pick a flower and the ground opens

A woman opens up
Her heart pick a flower, any flower

The hero says a bouquet in his hand
His smile goes to seed

When he pretends his hands are weeds
Everything

But the source wilts

19.

Earth so earthy in him so earthly
Or earthlike the little world accommodates
This sod he is so full

Of himself he calls himself "little fool"
With such tender love his tears turn
The garden into mud

Gods so godly above him so god-like
Throwing lightning and shining
In their faces he calls them

"those samples" and his laughter laughs
So heavenly or is it so heaven-like
The garden dries in his sigh

20.

Opinion and prayer
                or the onion's layers
Chorus and chaos
                or the curious rhyme
Tear away a peel
                and find a tear
Speak in one voice
                to keep measure or time

21.

Fate   the ditch
Smiles

Study nature to know

Yourself   a current
Cuts

Through the debris
& the debris

Gets carried away

22.

He smiles inside his own face and cries
Not the fear of monsters, but the fear that none exist
"Lightness" kept turning over and over in his mouth
Light then weight then light then weight

He cries inside his own face and smiles
"Monster" is a word and a word is a labyrinth
From one side you know your way about
From another side you no longer know your way about

"Fate"   he says it and it is like a torch
Chasing through the dark the person
Who wants to stay lost in the dark
Did he say "person"   Did he say "person"

23.

Desire grows a face and then the mirror makes sense
Of reflection's furious pursuit—the bells, the bells
Are shiny but they do not think when they ring
Stretching desire's face into its own atrocious mask
Where the mouth is a ditch that smiles

24.

Desire desires

The hero was taught and so he teaches
Tautology is the nature of

Fate
Whose breasts bell-like ring when she runs

And every tongue must say what it says

Calling me to myself, whoever
Me is

A name

25.

Clap clap clap goes the tongue
Clap clap clap

Breath is no wonderment
But being out of breath works hard
As a flower works hard
In the sunlight to open

Fate is the awful equation
That makes of one two
And makes of two one

    They open almost like eyes

Is what he thinks as he runs
Away from his own applause

    The flowers

puritanisms

1.

burn name as incense
other frugal economies
confess   the horizon
never points at me

2.

confess thoughts
I do not want thoughts
confess words
I spoke to think
words in others what I cannot think
in myself:

wilderness, bewilder

3.

study hooks
                    in nature
burr of the thistle &
                              thistle's
purple petals. This othering
forms thorns. A rose is also
wild

a finger says, Come &—

& grammar's
hook of the ampersand—

                    conjoin

4.

proud where I should feel shame
shameful where I should feel pride

great, gray goose
the one-strand river has no other side

5.

this diary meant   for other eyes
is how I am naked   when I arrive

this pudency, the selfish blank

this name, the overtakeless scent

6.

burn name for heat
spendthrift strategies
there is no image
for the same   a flame
suffices   I candle
or, I wick   this light
is the burden   this
light reveals this
light is sick

7.

I want you
about myself   to tell me
I'm wrong

these shallow deeps,
Narcissus—

look over the edge and see

8.

paper white

9.

obscure sun, or
the sun obscures

leaf's occult
property, eating
what does not
materially exist

my name walks around
with its mouth open

10.

smoke pours out the hole
I cannot write cruel enough
with enough cruelty I cannot

breathe I cannot bellow hard
enough to strike what sense
smolders into bright
flame to fill the hole with fire

11.

confess I speak
certainties I don't feel

these certain desires I
disguise in words to hide

me in myself where I cannot be
found

for example, in your ear
where in words seeming wise

I lusteth

12.

put me in my place
pull me out of myself
put me in

the hole
but the hole retreats

when you fill it

13.

this voice authors itself
a votive flame devoted
to light which destroys it
light whose devotion
it destroys with itself this
voice contains this idea
of itself utters what it knows
what later says I am past
tense on a page first glows

14.

. . . confess I confess to keep
wounded my wound confess
words keep open my eyes
I confess are wounds I see
through the wounds I confess . . .

15.

the jade plant crushing itself
against the living-room wall

sun comes through the window
but never fills in the whole glare

the lamp lit all day is one figure
as is the houseplant holding up a wall

16.

I cannot will this silence
Sapphic-gaps   I cannot
will these blanks

    song & stung

    time & twine

imperfectly rhyme
quite quietly

because I love
I write these love poems

17.

certainty in song
that limited guest
requires the heart's
syllable why why
grow intricate

18.

strike them and make them ring

but circumference resists these dents

margins bear a silence bare

dare this wren to sing she won't relent

19.

not in but am
house whose
windows only
inward open

20.

I am the hole I'm in

I fill the absence up

my idea about myself

solders air with abyss

21.

turn the inner outward
but the private part revolts

an hourglass swallows itself
and lets the sand spill out

22.

okay, I'll be ugly

the daylight is yellow all over
the helpless thing breathes, for how long
have I been establishing these distances
all inside me the poem is this bridge that must
create the distance it crosses

23.

a thing of beauty is a

thing

of beauty is forever

is forever a joy

a joy some thing

it a thing

beauty

24.

I buried my heart in the world
and walked away

but the world is not the earth

when the rainbow crumbled

I lived on crumbs

25.

they grew fat on nothing at my door
even confession a form

of pride pride forms

some sustenance I put down my book
and wasn't it right

to put down my book and let the birds

26.

supply the song for what ends in
drawing nearer the song for what
arrives as evanescence in reverse
confession confirms what cannot
remain the private part there is no
secret to abandon a language we
have no language for this in which
we startle the deer with our own
roots dangling from mouths the dirt
fecund coda of the most wounded
moist wound there is no song for what
ends in drawing nearer little bird here
is the crumb here is me too near myself
to see here little bird is the tiny crumb

overtakelessness

The corn grows at night—
    the pansy thinks—
a first fact satisfies
    until it thinks.

Until it sings, a fact
    grows certain—
rock-like root that cuts
    the rock in two.

*

Pansy as *pensée*
    revises its petal—
    pollen's adhesive
edits the mile

the bee dances
    its amendment—
    a pedagogy
simple—betray

the text's ample
    fact
    by dulling
the sickle.

*

gentlessness is a word
    to describe that
which must deny itself
    to exist.

It is a word I made up
    to describe
      to myself
myself and other fields.

    *

Nobody taught me
    this dance I dance—
I gather the air
    as weight around me—

(murmured rumors
    the pansies speak)

to pack my ears
    in pollen, I learned
      to shake
    my head
from side to side.

    *

Where did I bury it?—
    the sea, I mean, the
      seed?—

pansies grow pensive—

they point at the sun
    by opening
      their faces—

they open their faces
   to point at
      the sun—

where did I bury it?—
   the seed, I mean, the
      sea?—

*

The sun rises twice—
   less gentle in the other
field, overtakeless

in mine. The pansies sing
   their nursery rhyme:
a fact is a fact,
   roots dig, tendrils twine,

this sun is the sun
   we call ours, I call mine—
the corn grows at night
   but where is the night?—

a song the sun sings to dull
   itself down—gentle

other, right here is where—
   the day begins, and then:

*

The bee-maidens speak
  a minor prophecy
    true

when gorged on honey—

but when hungry
    the bee-maidens lie—
time is never open,
    time is always closed—

in words there is no
    difference—
the poem is a hermetic
    delight.

*

I tend a fear I call a field—
    pansy glanced
at the passing plow—
    shaking my head

gentlessly, side to side,
    sifting thoughts
to sow seeds. In fear—
    is it in fear?—

the roots grip downward.
    I keep my eyes closed.
I sow these seeds
    when I say *no*—

Shaking my head—
    I know, I do not know—
from side to side
    the stem reaches

upward, it bends, it follows
    the sun—it reaches up
and bends—in what?

I shake my head
    in what?—
disbelief?—

*

The eye pushes this plow
    across the page
but here the sillion won't
    shine—

pansies is a word
    seven stones long—
a word made severe
    in a line—

when the bees build themselves
    inside the hive
there is no exit—

they sting each
    other
to survive.

*

beside
  the white chickens

glazed
  with rain water

a
  red wheelbarrow

so
  much depends upon

*

Sweet rural song—
    each day lasts forever
        but forever
is not long—

Rust sings a hole in another's
    song—
wild-carrot's lace-work
    in metal

the sun heats but does not
    warm—
blade of plow, straps' leather
    thongs—

*

I pull the plow behind me.
It cuts a line I cannot see.
    It opens up the sea

    behind me as I work.
How do I know? I hear
the waves crash on rocks

that they are there, brine
in the air the gulls cry out
    hunger, why

    are they so sad?—
the sea?—the sea?—
It is a long line behind me

using itself to point at
itself—it also points away—
    using itself to point away.

*

The bee hurts
    philosophy—

or is it thought
    that stings

the bee? I think
    therefore—

*

So much depends upon
    what
so much depends—

this what behind the eyes—
    this what?—this
field?—

this grass that dreams
    its own roots—
this moon, or this cloud-
    covered moon—

this what that is
    the moon-lit filled
night that is

when the eyes blink, that is—
    when I blink my eyes—
I feel it, this

weight that is this painfulness
    in both shoulders—
yes, the straps.

*

    a hive hums a
        work-song

    dance maps the
        wild-flower

field maddens in
    paper hive

where there is
    no exit—

I am; therefore,
    this sting—

*

I confess I have lived
much of my life in the ideal
    crisis. I think

of this place as a place.
What is it that is too obvious
    to say? Is it that

the pansies hold no
elections? The sun pulls up
    as if on strings

the green questions
of stems. There are other forms
    of legislation, the bees drone:

*

Wild-carrot with a purple wound
    the petals spin around

        their center, grave
point—what quickens the heart—

the axis of the flower is—
    well, I won't say it—.
        It seems to turn around itself,
in itself, upon itself, a spiral

pulling itself down into—
    I don't want to
        say what is—
is missing.

        *

The hour ate the song
    just as the water swallowed
the stone just as the sun ate
    the moon just as the moon bit
the night it could not consume

the whole night. The earth shrugs
    and turns away, blue-
shouldered earth, helpless blue
    shoulders, turning away
the same motion as turning to—

        *

What sings a song wants
    what in a song

sings—
a field is a form of bankruptcy

turning itself over to find
    debris—pot-shard,
        arrowhead,
husk of the opened seed.

*

Myself is a word to describe
    this field that I cannot see
the end of, this field I tend,
    burying the dead in rows,

burying the sea, burying seeds.
    If there is another horizon
I have not seen it. I have not learned
    to see it. This pebble? It's a point.

*

I see why the horizon doesn't
    step near. Evanescence
isn't fear. Distance
    requires recognition.

There is that tree that turns on
    the lathe to make for the hand
a gentle handle. I is a splinter
    for which *selfishness* is a gentle word.

*

The grass is not the only one
who dreams. I found myself
out where I was hiding

in the grass I was hiding away
from the grass in myself.
    I knew no one who could answer

    the question I could not ask.
My heart made its point.
Frantic with what does not exist.

    The whole field grips downward.
I mean my fingers in the dirt.
I mean my heart has a point

and a point is that
which has no
    part.

*

    I kept the tree in
mind and turned
  the tree around
    until

   it fit.
  I love thinking.
I love this skeptic's
    lathe.

Open your throat,
poet. What is the
    leaf-dappled
        light.

*

This field, this
    leaky boat—

the sea seeps
    in—

springs up and
    in, and—

under the grain—
    beneath

the seeds—we
    don't

sift fingers
    through

amber waves—
    we learn

to drown, or
    we sink.

*

These songs are skeptics' songs—
　　the pansies applaud
by quickly closing
　　their faces—

How break the spell? Say,
　　I'm weary. Say,
the blade's edge grew dull.
　　Say, the sound I am

listening to is too small.
　　How is it I can speak
all these words with my mouth
　　pressed against the ground?

I have spent a life in the field
　　turning it over to learn
how to turn myself over and lie
　　in the field face down.

*

Teeth are this poor man's plow
　　cutting the music into rows,
dulled down by the dirt,
　　this face is this poor man's tool,
tilling the earth by trilling the song,
　　melody mumming the blossom
back into itself, the initial seed
　　broken apart by what it cannot

help, this force that confesses
　　itself, that says I from the broken
mouth, that confesses this mouth
　　has always been mine, this shovel,
this mouth, singing the flower
　　back to fact, rock-like fact,
so much depends upon the fact as it
　　betrays itself, the green point
mocking its own source, the field
　　that is nothing, field that is nowhere,
found only by the green points breaking
　　through themselves to exist, green
points that deny themselves, a point
　　being that which has no heart, a line
being breathless length, these green
　　points in a line, a line that points away
from me wherever I am me, muttering
　　what is it to be about something, what

is it to be　　to be about　　what is it
　　to be something　　to be about something
what is it to be　　to be about　　what is
　　it to be　　about what is about　　what

romanticisms

Mortal oddment, there's no wish in the blood
But beat, but stay gift-strong, but make demands
To keep within veins this ore's diffuse gold,
These voices that know without being known—
These voices that riddle thought with herself,
Ridicule thought in her flimsy eternal
Gowns a child can tear in half with a breath—
That chorus arterial, unbribable,
Blowing song through self as a child blows
A dandelion apart—

                All those weeds?—
Thistle's down and thistle's thorn, dumb yellow
Globes below that bind grass to their hollow creed,
Wind's meager flute, sere song, the whole field's late
Doom? Heart-blood? Voices, you? That's my portrait?—

Her waxen seal: sparrow on a broken lyre.
Her broken seal: a sparrow broken.
The page unfolds, paradise creased with desire—
And a scent that breathes her breath shaken
By my own shaking hand. Read each word twice
To find that empty cell gorged with honey
That never sates, that never satisfies,
But makes desire desirous—Tell me,
Why did I laugh? . . . pressing the pale page
To my lips to pretend the white wrist's pulse
Pressed back, quickening. Poor fever's rage
Where paper is person and person falls
To ground so gently, like a leaf, like a leaf—
Broken bird, blank bird, sing, sing. Here's the sheaf.

Breathe the sunny air, but the storm storms
There in the mote in the wind catching the light
Just so, in gnat-wing and dust, in pollen up-blown,
Until the cloud clouds as the lid closes an eye—
But some are so dark, some eyes so dark,
They stare out blind from beneath the lids'
Skin-thin veil. The sleeper sleeps in her dark
Mist, hearing, not-hearing, the katydid's
Verdant clicks from out the poplar's foliage
Above the chain-link fence. Breathe the sunny
Air, but the night fevers to its very edge
This fevered life. Put the dumb moon in the eye
And the nerve-riddle cools, calms, it is so full—
Moss-song, fungal dirge, elegy and dung-beetle.

I kept repeating, repeating, kept re—
To repair, to repair my, or not my—*the*
Mind's bower, but whose—who mines urgency—
Or whose mind regrets all those violets rooted
In violence—or I only mean thought, in thought,
Not violence, thinking, and the stupid leaf
Unfolding, mine, mine, mind. Here's the plot
All untended: Psyche and, and—some thief
Unnamed—no, some unnamed leaf, and the sun,
Yes, only the sun that through open eyes
Turns the livid leaf green. Not leaf. Meant wound—
Or is it wind, is it wind that split in half by
A gnat, by a blade of grass, always heals its gale—
What is the wound that is being healed, healed—

Sing the earth's melody back to the earth—
Fill the clod again with song so this clod
Fills with silence, this clod in silence birthed—.
But still, there sodden sits the half-rot root
Thought digs deeper down to that ideal pain
To drink (as a dog drinks from fen to slake
Its hunting thirst)—thought that pursues the man
Who thinks until thinking dies, water that shakes
When the eye blinks, when in darkness complete
The poet fills his mouth with names he cannot
Speak, but murmurs to himself that secret
The flies murmur within the flowers they haunt—
There is none, there is none (and the cloud
Of gnats agrees): aster, musk-rose, flood.

But this logic stutters as the fool in fever
Mutters to the fly to cease its endless
Circuit around the sunlit chamber
And regard dying with attention more precise.
Easy to break the vase—so heavy, head
Of peony grown pendent within its scent,
Some child's head in the dying day's honeyed heat
Asleep above the book to which he bends
Slowly down until his lip on the page wakes him . . .
Just like that the vase breaks, just a fly
Landing on a petal shatters the whole dream.
But how shatter the shard? Flatter the shy
Heart? Push the finger down on what gleams
Until the finger bleeds? What then? Stifle
Cry, staunch drop, find crueler ways to be cruel?

Be generous—. But the nettle's bloom bitters
Its lesson deep into the thumb's lovely
Incaution, and the rose thrown in the gutter
Still casts out its scent so sweet it's sickly,
Almost shapely, love's ghastly prepossession.
I hoped to die before spring came again,
Then the dung beetle made its confession.
Then the pillow kept my silhouette's stain—.
I rose as if I never had risen—.
Be cautious—. But the letter lays bare
Those marks her own hand pressed through words
Onto the page below this page, where
White on white makes present all past, absurd
Legibility, as grief notes grief,
The colors of the sky, and the sky itself—.

Gnats breed, mind broods, a cloud in the air
Breathes out one breath until the cloud is gone,
And the sun pours down heat in glaring hours
That prisms wings as thought prisons song.
The grass dreams other dreams than those the crickets
Conspire—dreams of being those taut lyre-strings
Pulled up to the sun despite the thicket's
Maze; but the lyre is in the sun, and sings
To itself some glaring song that withers all
Other ears. Do they—"wailful"—mourn? The wind
Construes its own cell gorged on dismal
Nothing by nothing marked. Not wind—mind—
And the rainbow-flash sprung out the gnats' glass
Wings marks the eye's prayer; it shows it what it lacks.

The Cricket and the Grasshopper

The senseless leaf in the fevered hand
Grows hot, near blood-heat, but never grows
Green. Weeks ago the dove's last cooing strain
Settled silent in the nest to brood slow
Absence from song. The dropped leaf cools
On the uncut grass, supple still, still green,
Twining still these fingers as they listless pull
The tangle straight until the tangle tightens
And the hand is caught, another fallen leaf.
The poetry of the earth never ceases
Ceasing—one blade of grass denies belief
Until its mere thread bears the grasshopper's
Whole weight, and the black cricket sings unseen,
Desire living in a hole beneath the tangle's green.

—think of the earth; and the river is not
Some giant's nerve the stippled cut-throats
Swim thoughtfully in; and the merest tufts
Of dandelion seeds in thoughtless air caught
Are not the unravished bride's relenting dress
Where in the quiet field she waits. Enough
Mereness: forgotten hands holding depthless
Tones. The articulate worm in the dark cave
Knows the earth's song: *nervous water, damsel-*
fly, shadow on the river; brides wander,
blown weeds in serest field, mouths that fill
with water; damselfly, nervous water . . .
There it is the blown bride wanders and laments.
There the gaping mouth chants a song called appetite.

The grass is and isn't some flame's waiting bed—
I saw the nude bride lean back in the grass,
Legs askance, one hand holding above her head
A lantern, a waterfall, the illuminating gas.
Her face fell outside the frame. Those flowers
Leaned in the direction she'd look, if she had eyes
To look, she'd look in the direction those flowers
Pointed, sky-ward arc that bends, arc that in dry
Earth ends. My eye hurt from all its dumb looking.
My dumb eye in its hurt looking. I like
To think I made this choice to not open
The door, even if the door had no knob, I like
To think I made a choice to put my hand
On my throat to hear my throat as my own.

The folds unfolded become a fan; that dark
Line curving so gentle before nothing cuts
Its arc, unfolds as does the wing of a lark
In a child's puppet play, slat by feathered slat
Until the wing undone the bird is pulled
Into the sky by a wire. Look up—
There on the ceiling the rainbow fools
With light through cut glass thrown, slight lisp
Of the blue fly's slow circle, and on the cup's lip
The print of your lips, lips that when the fan's crisp
Edge dips I see part slightly as if—, glimpse
Quickly denied my longing, shameless glare,
By the silk print: sparrow on a broken lyre.

Not heroes who stepped through the mortal fact
The field in thistle and writhing weed writes,
No shining proof of the prayed-for god's invoked
Step interfering, not heroes—   hermits
blind who count their wealth by touching what shines
and in the mind's crumpled ledger scratch
the changeless number's wretched *mine, mine*—
Not heroes, not hermits—   the poet's lit match
Whose brief light lights the matterless matter,
Sparse line's struggle to bear the wild song's
Burden whole before leaves wilt and scatter
Darkly the dark notes of the nightingale wronged,
Tereu, tereu—   not poet, a page to tear
From book when a poem fails to name the stars stars

Deep in wood the hermit thrush sings drip drip
Drop, the song a child hears and wanders long
Into the wood singing her song, drop drop
Drip, a song the hermit thrush hears and sings
Along, drip drop drip drop, the song a child
Hears and sings along as she wanders deep
Where shadows brood beneath fern fronds unfurled
And water drips from a rock drop drip drop
A song the hermit thrush hears and hearing nears
And broods in song, drip drop drip, a child sings
Along as water drips from a rock a tear-
Shaped drip that is the wandering child's song
She sings drip drop a song the hermit thrush hears
And out the fond shadow the bird singing nears

modernisms

In a Station of the Metro

Peace fell on the dim lands a sort of abstraction
The metronome counted one petal after another
So the petals fell as or in some music
This song needs no breath just an apparition
With a mouth open and eyes and eyes
The wet smear of eyes beneath pink
Petals in excess of the window frame's bright
Yellow square and yes spring gathers right now
The moisture from my breath up into clouds
Whose downpour makes of the plum-tree in blossom
A diminishing crowd for which the natural symbol
Refuses to exist a plain blue gem on a pin
Faces glowing within the stone like flowers
Within the stone like flaws the mind turns inward
Turns inward its tangle of wet black boughs
A knot pulled tight so tight it ceases to be

A knot yes I'll say it a knot that becomes angelic
Another example everywhere seen of the angelic
Gears toothless and without cogs a sort of mist
That turns the other gear by drifting through it
As just now through my eye drifts that storm-
Battered tree whose broken-petal pocked bark
Asks of me a question my mouth can't speak
Like a river that dives underground just there
There where the animals thirst the most
A desert fox say or say a toad or let's speak more simply
About a plum which bursts through its own explosion
Into being and hangs there so ponderously
As if as if not concerned with innocence or

Gravity or other acute angles as they evaporate
Into this poem O no am I speaking again again about
Dim lands these dim dim lands of of peace

No Man's Land

The world no longer tears me, so I don't write poems.
This sentence is one I often tell myself.
It's not like being self-aware on the page
Is a new trick, or the poem growing aware of itself
As it's being written, discovering
Unsuspected mines from which lost children
Bring back to their hovels rubies and diamonds.
A dove drops a dress down from the hazel tree.
This chair I'm sitting in, made from marzipan,
Is food for thought, a thought such as *shake*
And shiver, little tree, throw gold and silver down
On me. The sun comes in through the window
So clear I can almost forget the glass is only sugar
The deer lick and bound away to nothing.

"The mind is its own malady." I wrote that line myself,
Even published it. Self-reference marks irony,
So I'm told. But irony is when you know something
About me I don't know about myself. Sorry.
I promised myself I would be less didactic: me,
Your teacher. That's what the paystub says: your teacher.
Let me erase everything on this white board.
It's named "Ghost Duster," the eraser. Isn't that funny?
This white fluorescent blank is bright like still water.
Narcissus kept notes on all the water he tasted, traveling
Throughout the lands, ignoring those who fell in love
With him only to distract him, keeping bliss at bay,
Searching for that spring so pure its waters taste like
Nothing at all. He kept his notebook tied to his belt
Many nymphs tried to loosen, tried to loosen

His limbs. Digitally archived, anyone can see,
In his own hand, what he wrote—but unless you speak
The language, as I don't, you'll need, as I did,
The translation. *Like Dryope's tears.*
That's my favorite. You know how you can write
Such words? You need to find Dryope, poor soul,
Changed into a tree, only one in the whole world,
And then you put your tongue to its bark
And wait, maybe forever, for her to cry.

But who has forever? This poplar, most likely
Grew from a seed, maybe a cutting, and the vibration
I felt in the trunk was only the wind far above
In the leaves. Poplars, really, they're a nuisance.
Yes, the leaves in the wind can play in the silence
Of a single note and when the sun flashes the underside
Of every leaf at once all that remains is forgetting,
Some variation of death, but grown old
It sheds its limbs with the slightest gust. Did you hear
That crack as of distant thunder
But the sky is cloudless? Did you hear the one
About the mother who lost her arms and her child
Kept asking to be picked up?—it's a bad joke.

So bad I've kept trying to forget it, every word,
And so I've learned you can't teach yourself how
To forget. Teacher, where are you?
Let me take the test again and I promise
I'll fill in the answers you gave me:
Dark circles beside all of the *all of the above*. What?
I'm still taking the test? I thought I stopped
When I put the pencil down and walked into the woods
Following this trail made of bread crumbs.
I remember Odysseus like he was yesterday—

Carrying his oar on his shoulder inland
Waiting for a stranger to compliment him
On his winnowing fan. I've been walking—
I want to say my whole life, but that can't be
True—my hands held out in front of me, my hands
Held out in front of me, but no one has yet
Mistaken them for a winnowing fan, no one,
Not even when careless I sat on a granary floor
Raking my hands through the grain
As through a child's hair. And if I say I think
I hear a clock as if ticking always in the air,
What of it? The chaff blew away and
My wind-blown hair like a war-flag pointed after it.

The New World

Push in the push-pin right here in this blank
This blank a little effort mars
Emptiness into something more empty
Empty as the air when the drone ceases
A single note thrills nothing's whole system
A kind of star-map before any stars existed
Don't sigh it's just a hole in a page
A hole in a page just a kind of beginning
Before time begins again its infinite counting
On infinite fingers of infinite stars
Departure on every side yes I read the report
On abandonment while in my office eating lunch
Every point departs ever faster from every point
Nothing verges into nothingness even now forever
Absent territories grow forever more vast

*

Data suggest the angelic hierarchies
Drone ceaselessly a single note
The x-ray telescopes record as endless beige
Endless as the low-cost carpet of a state
Education years ago I complained
Memory no longer works no poet wanders
Into a city and begins to sing that song
That includes us among the dust bereft
Now that the Tamer of Horses has died
I've never forgotten what I was told
A nameless man sits at a desk in a nameless city

Reading forever the same book
To keep near it despite its desire to disappear
Give him a push-pin and he can push it in
Push it in any page as deep as strength
Page as deep as strength allows
And by memory the nameless man recites
Each letter the pin he pushed pushed through
I know I've seen the book
I've seen the book every page of it every letter of
Every page is a hole

*

Once upon a time my wife told me to stop
Writing poems about writing poems
And for a present she gave me a box of pins
Happy birthday she said may this new year
Pierce you with anxieties more legible
Time will tell
Time will tell the ice to melt
Ice caves to melt and fog the pleasure-dome's glass
So the threshers flail in mist the doubtful grain
In mist the chaffy grain in the sacred grove
Hasn't exactly turned rotten yet
Some offering left long ago on some altar
Some prayer no one thought to teach me
The prayer motion no one taught me how
To build from nothing an altar
An empty page pinned to a desk I'm waiting
Pinned to the desk just waiting a page
Of instructions and a set of tools
Of tools kept high on a shelf in the air
Just waiting for the tools to fall

*

What do you see through the little hole
When you look through it
Is it what they see when they open their eyes
The animals when they open their eyes on the
Open the denial of the
Open that devours that gnaws
Distance swallowing itself to grow immense
Unable to run faster than what runs always
Faster run away but
Running away only runs closer to the—
Or do you see as I see when I hold the pin-hole
Up a field of gravel stands
Tractor treads trailing like tresses behind
A field of flowers no not flowers
Field where the test-blast blew the houses down
Radiation a glowing gown the wind wears
The wind wears the poppies' radiant glow
When over the graveyard it too grievously blows
Keening it cuts away the margins
Keening it cuts as does the passing plow cut
One more petal from the petal-less whole
A bare stem looks like a
Looks like a thread holding up a hole
A hole instead of a head just a thread holds up
The hole don't sigh
What do you see through the little hole
When you look through it what do you see

*

Ignore almost
The drone of the man reciting
By memory the page
He holds up the sun
Pours through each hole
Letter by letter the
Sun on his desk the whole
Alphabet a thousand suns
On his desk ignore
Almost the drone of the
Man by memory reciting
The sun

*

Then friend will you see as I see
Past the described fields all inviting you in
Across the graveyards and over the aviaries
Beyond the chalk cliffs where swallows
Where swallows nest in holes
Nest in holes the sun never quite fills
Past the always filling never full sea
There where three men and a woman gather
They gather in their robes
In their robes before a stone
And two of the men watch intently anxiously
As the third bends down to trace his fingers
On the letters carved in the stone
Traces his fingers on the letters he cannot read

Friend so he remains forever silent
And don't sigh forever the woman looks
Looks away looks down as if she sees
In the field a hole no one else can see
A flaw only her own little pin-hole
A little tear in the canvas and without a tear
She spends eternity watching
Watching disappear what all it is that
All it is that disappears

Paperwhite

I consulted with myself about it
Praying for and laboring after an awakening sense
This ghost chose my head to do its thinking in
A kind of arcadia where the painter puts light
On the water perfectly despite the tremors
Of the always filling never full sea
Or this salt and absence of the backward glance

*

A certain quality of light in the air visible
For a day or two when spring finally opens,
I look backward and become the pillar of salt
Apology looks back through itself to see
A snake in the grass the color of the grass
Or the garden hose swallowed by what it feeds
This strange rite of wanting to say something simple

*

Only to find my own image out ahead of me singing
A brittle pastoral grows supple as it goes blank
Wind gone but the grass bends over still blown
As sweetness falls away from what is sweet
And 'this' becomes a word that forgets what follows
Delirious judgment separating shadows from shades
A poppy just now full-blown and memory all 'this'

Portrait

You have to walk so close to the mirror
Before your breath clouds the image
You need to get a running start
You need to get a running start
To break through the refrain into repetition
As exile's continuous form forms the same
Words twice thrush thrush
Drab bird unseen in the dark dark's underbrush
Sung from the yeasty mouth

*

From within the cloud the voice sings
The voice is a singing cloud
You have to walk so close to breath
Before you find the mirror
And then beginning looks just like
Beginning looks just like
What doesn't know how to complete itself
Otherwise
What is there in saying *house bridge fountain*

*

bridge fountain gate jug
jug fruit-tree window there I said them
All and every all's this same
Cloud's faulty tower is this same
Cloud's broken column trying to make a point
About breath by mentioning breath
I stand so close to the surface of the thing
I am dumb because I make myself dumb
And then the apples go mute

*

Jug jug
Make no noise
Who will find you in the middle of your breath
And keep whole all you want broken
Someone becomes
Someone again it must be done
Mouth scaring bird from its ever more hidden nest
A surface seems to know something about
Depth depth cannot know about itself

*

Right toward the mirror
Watch it fly as sometimes it does fly
Breath and every cloud
The sky has gotten a running start
It's why the apples ripen even though they hurt
The sky's running start
Let panic return and stand very still

You have to stand very still
Before what is wounded turns around and nears

*

A note plays in the dark
Plays all by itself in the dark just a note
Just a note called escape
What I'm telling you is what I cannot say
Otherwise this
Intimate breath is just another maze
The sun disappears
Inside the apple I mean there is a mirror
In a cloud and right there is your answer

Portrait (After Arcimboldo)

I made this self all by myself
I drove this nail into the wall myself
I stained the wood's grain I planed the wood myself
I wrote the book on the shelf I made myself

The very fact is the face of the made thing
A fact is that it's hard to see the face from within the thing
I want to say the face is a thinking thing
But the fact is that a face only thinks it is a thinking thing

A spine on a book and legs on a chair
And legs on a table and arms on a chair
A vase's neck a cup's lip a water-ring on a chair's
Arm made by a body all disappeared whose weight
      pressed itself down into a—

Who can know and also not know what he knows?—
A feeling called music but music only a word he used
      to know
And empty rings and bracelets and scattered beads all
      forms of knowing
Absence as the finger fills the shape by which it's known

What I am inside of I cannot see that I cannot see
I cannot see inside myself to see
Memory and song or even a bone is a faith that says
      "Do not see"
Or a tree that holds its blossoms' husks all winter long
      is what I cannot see

Not one object exists in this song
Not even the singer as he sings this song

It's bad advice to tell those without a face to sing and
never stop singing
The voice inside the mask but it's the mask that sings

An anger song a war song a love song all must be
pursued to become real
In ardor must be pursued to become real
There was a bird in the deep wood's all gloom that sang
as if real
But only when the poet shouted away did the bird
become real

It sounds like a joke, but I told my face to go away
A child might know to close his eyes so that his face
goes away
But the inside of the face is this darkness from which
one can't run away
Nor does running help that much when you want to
run away

It helps to be less than beautiful it helps to have on the
lips a livid scar
Demonstrating heaven is a form of accuracy legible
only in a scar
And angels differ from monsters only in the capacity of
monsters to bear scars
But an angel can cut through your body with its body
and leave no scar

I bring up angels only to distract myself from the
starless dome
The bankrupt planetarium's silent projector beneath
the blank dome

But I sit in the folding chair anyway looking up at
    the dome
On which the fake stars never appear and the heroes
    vacate their theater's ancient dome

This poem is just another song not meant for hearing
The first cause spins the furthermost globe with its
    thumb all calloused from eternity's hearing
And I drum my thumb against the wood too quiet for
    anyone's hearing
Even my own   I simply feel a pressure that replaces
    hearing

I want a teacher
There's an emptiness around which I must gather
    objects but no one will teach
Me what objects those should be   no one will teach
Me what is the made thing but a fact no else's face
    can teach

My face—
What work must be done I want to say some words
    about a face any face
Mine which seems to be an action a face
Should do words should come out of a face

But these words all come out by hand and this face is
    the hand's accident
This face in which the lion starves because the swallow
    starves, an accidental
Sympathy or rhythm that prolongs the moment of
    contemplation into an accident
The mind cannot avoid its own dispersal into accident

And that accident is my face, see: on a doorstep, a
    crumb;
See: the crease of the dog-eared page; see: a broken
    string;
See: snake's skin, bookmark, and this broken cocoon
See: this shaken pollen's blush still mars this blank
    page;
See: the curve of the deer's tender haunch, and the
    plastic hoop
Through which the child blows her incandescent bubble;
See: the ruined stairs, the spokeless banister, the railing
Screwed into the empty wall; See: sea foam and those
    curtains
Of pine dust blown yellow into the sea; See: this
    slender stalk
And the chaff fallen from the winnowed germ, and the
    seed all blown away,
That placed above my body holds my body down

Acknowledgments

Thank you to the editors who published portions of these series in journals, and to those who published whole series as chapbooks. I feel quick gratitude at the kindness.

"monadisms: a proem" is dedicated to Tirzah Goldenberg and Rico Moore.

"a short treatise on the nature of the gods": Sections 2 and 3 first appeared in *Cell Poems*. The Argotist (UK) published the poem as an online chapbook; thank you to Rebecca Beachy for providing the cover art. The quotation in section 16 is from René Char, and in 22 is from Emily Dickinson.

"heroisms": Thank you to Timothy Donnelly for publishing the whole poem on the *Boston Review* website. *Poor Claudia* published the same as a chapbook; thank you Drew Scott Swanhaugen and Marshall Walker Lee. Sections 4 and 5 were part of the Academy of American Poets *Poem-a-Day* site.

"puritanisms": Thank you to Andrew Feld at *Seattle Review* for publishing the entire series. Sections 2, 4, and 5 were published at *Cell Poems*.

"overtakelessness": Many thanks to all the fine folk at Spork Press —Jake Levine, Drew Burk, and Andrew Shuta—for publishing this series as a chapbook.

"romanticisms": Thank you to *Poetry, The Mayo Review*, and *The Journal*.

"In a Station of the Metro": Thank you to Christian Wiman, Don Share, and Christina Pugh for publishing this piece in *Poetry*, with an accompanying interview.

"No Man's Land" appeared in Riddle Fence. Thank you to Joshua Trotter, Leigh Kotsilidis, Jeramy Dodds, and Gabe Foreman.

"The New World": appeared in *Blackbox Manifold* (UK). Thank you to Alex Houen.

"Paperwhite" is *for* and *after* Susan Howe. Thank you to Zach Barocas for publishing this on *The Cultural Society* website.

"Portrait" was published at the Academy of American Poets *Poem-a-Day* site. Thank you Alex Dmitrov.

"Portrait (After Arcimboldo)" first appeared in *The Idaho Review*. To all the editors there, and those at Boise State in general, ongoing thanks.

*

Without the patience and good advice of many friends these poems would be less. I owe especial thanks to Martin Corless-Smith, Sally Keith, Srikanth Reddy, and Sasha Steensen. Gratitude also to James Galvin, Matthew Cooperman, Aby Kaupang, Gordon Hadfield, Sarah Sloane, Leslee Becker, Louann Reid, Stephan Weiler, and Ann Gill. Thank you to everyone at Tupelo Press for the ongoing work in and toward poetry. The gift of a Monfort Professorship made the completion of this manuscript possible; thank you to the Monfort family for such support.

Other books from Tupelo Press

See our complete list at www.tupelopress.org